Memory verse(s) from today's reading:

How this passage can be applied to my life:

MY BIBLE STUDY
JOURNAL

KeyNotes

BARBOUR
PUBLISHING

Published by Barbour Publishing, Inc., P.O. Box 719, Uhrichsville, Ohio 44683
www.barbourbooks.com

Our mission is to publish and distribute inspirational products offering exceptional value and biblical encouragement to the masses.

 Member of the
Evangelical Christian
Publishers Association

Printed in China.

Study to shew thyself

approved unto God,

a workman that

needeth not to be ashamed,

rightly dividing the word of truth.

2 TIMOTHY 2:15 KJV

Let the word of Christ dwell in you richly as you teach
and admonish one another with all wisdom.

COLOSSIANS 3:16 NIV

Key Bible verses: _____

_____

_____

_____

_____

_____

_____

_____

_____

_____

Date:

Notes: _____

_____

_____

_____

_____

_____

_____

_____

_____

_____

_____

_____

_____

How this passage can be applied to my life:

_____
_____
_____
_____
_____
_____
_____
_____
_____
_____
_____
_____
_____

Memory verse(s) from today's reading:

_____
_____
_____
_____
_____
_____
_____
_____
_____
_____
_____
_____

When you received the word of God. . .you accepted it not as the word of men,
but as it actually is, the word of God, which is at work in you who believe.

1 THESSALONIANS 2:13 NIV

Key Bible verses: _____

Date:

Notes: _____

How this passage can be applied to my life:

_____
_____
_____
_____
_____
_____
_____
_____
_____
_____
_____
_____
_____

Memory verse(s) from today's reading:

_____
_____
_____
_____
_____
_____
_____
_____
_____
_____
_____
_____

As the hart panteth after the water brooks,
so panteth my soul after thee, O God.

PSALM 42:1 KJV

Key Bible verses: _____

_____
_____
_____
_____
_____
_____
_____
_____
_____

Date:

Notes: _____

_____
_____
_____
_____
_____
_____
_____
_____
_____
_____
_____

How this passage can be applied to my life:

_____
_____
_____
_____
_____
_____
_____
_____
_____
_____
_____

Memory verse(s) from today's reading:

_____
_____
_____
_____
_____
_____
_____
_____
_____
_____
_____
_____

"Therefore everyone who hears these words of Mine and acts on them, may be compared to a wise man who built his house on the rock."

MATTHEW 7:24 NASB

Key Bible verses: _____

Date: _____

Notes: _____

How this passage can be applied to my life:

_____

_____

_____

_____

_____

_____

_____

_____

_____

_____

Memory verse(s) from today's reading:

_____

_____

_____

_____

_____

_____

_____

_____

_____

_____

_____

And Jesus answered. . . "But one thing is needed,
and Mary has chosen that good part, which will not be taken away from her."

LUKE 10:41–42 NKJV

Key Bible verses: _____

Date: _____

Notes: _____

How this passage can be applied to my life:

_____
_____
_____
_____
_____
_____
_____
_____
_____

Memory verse(s) from today's reading:

_____
_____
_____
_____
_____
_____
_____
_____
_____
_____

The things which you learned and received and heard and saw in me, these do,
and the God of peace will be with you.

PHILIPPIANS 4:9 NKJV

Key Bible verses: _____

_____

_____

_____

_____

_____

_____

_____

_____

_____

_____

Date:

Notes: _____

_____

_____

_____

_____

_____

_____

_____

_____

_____

_____

_____

How this passage can be applied to my life:

_____
_____
_____
_____
_____
_____
_____
_____
_____
_____

Memory verse(s) from today's reading:

_____
_____
_____
_____
_____
_____
_____
_____
_____
_____
_____
_____

Jesus answered and said to them, "This is the work of God,
that you believe in Him whom He sent."

JOHN 6:29 NKJV

Key Bible verses:

_____

Date:

Notes:

How this passage can be applied to my life:

_____

_____

_____

_____

_____

_____

_____

_____

_____

_____

Memory verse(s) from today's reading:

_____

_____

_____

_____

_____

_____

_____

_____

_____

_____

_____

Quicken me according to thy word.

PSALM 119:154 KJV

Key Bible verses: _____

_____
_____
_____
_____
_____
_____
_____
_____
_____
_____

Date:

Notes: _____

_____
_____
_____
_____
_____
_____
_____
_____
_____
_____
_____
_____
_____

How this passage can be applied to my life:

_____
_____
_____
_____
_____
_____
_____
_____
_____
_____
_____

Memory verse(s) from today's reading:

_____
_____
_____
_____
_____
_____
_____
_____
_____
_____
_____

For no prophecy was ever made by an act of human will,
but men moved by the Holy Spirit spoke from God.

2 PETER 1:21 NASB

Key Bible verses: _____

_____

_____

_____

_____

_____

_____

_____

_____

_____

Date:

Notes: _____

_____

_____

_____

_____

_____

_____

_____

_____

_____

_____

_____

_____

_____

How this passage can be applied to my life:

_____

_____

_____

_____

_____

_____

_____

_____

_____

_____

_____

Memory verse(s) from today's reading:

_____

_____

_____

_____

_____

_____

_____

_____

_____

_____

_____

O send out Your light and Your truth, let them lead me;
let them bring me to Your holy hill and to Your dwelling places.

PSALM 43:3 NASB

Date:

Key Bible verses: _____

_____
_____
_____
_____
_____
_____
_____
_____
_____
_____

Notes: _____

_____
_____
_____
_____
_____
_____
_____
_____
_____
_____
_____
_____
_____

How this passage can be applied to my life:

_____
_____
_____
_____
_____
_____
_____
_____
_____
_____
_____

Memory verse(s) from today's reading:

_____
_____
_____
_____
_____
_____
_____
_____
_____
_____
_____

Be strong and do not give up, for your work will be rewarded.

2 CHRONICLES 15:7 NIV

Key Bible verses: _____

_____
_____
_____
_____
_____
_____
_____
_____
_____
_____

Date: _____

Notes: _____

_____
_____
_____
_____
_____
_____
_____
_____
_____
_____
_____
_____
_____

How this passage can be applied to my life:

_____
_____
_____
_____
_____
_____
_____
_____
_____
_____
_____

Memory verse(s) from today's reading:

_____
_____
_____
_____
_____
_____
_____
_____
_____
_____
_____

For you were once darkness, but now you are light in the Lord.

EPHESIANS 5:8 NIV

Key Bible verses: _____

_____
_____
_____
_____
_____
_____
_____
_____
_____

Notes: _____

_____
_____
_____
_____
_____
_____
_____
_____
_____
_____
_____
_____

Date: _____

How this passage can be applied to my life:

_____

_____

_____

_____

_____

_____

_____

_____

_____

_____

Memory verse(s) from today's reading:

_____

_____

_____

_____

_____

_____

_____

_____

_____

_____

For the earnest expectation of the creation eagerly waits
for the revealing of the sons of God.

ROMANS 8:19 NKJV

Key Bible verses: _____

_____

_____

_____

_____

_____

_____

_____

_____

_____

_____

Date:

Notes: _____

_____

_____

_____

_____

_____

_____

_____

_____

_____

_____

_____

_____

How this passage can be applied to my life:

_____
_____
_____
_____
_____
_____
_____
_____
_____
_____

Memory verse(s) from today's reading:

_____
_____
_____
_____
_____
_____
_____
_____
_____
_____
_____

I thank Christ Jesus our Lord who has enabled me,
because He counted me faithful.

1 TIMOTHY 1:12 NKJV

Key Bible verses: _____

_____

_____

_____

_____

_____

_____

_____

_____

_____

_____

Date:

Notes: _____

_____

_____

_____

_____

_____

_____

_____

_____

_____

_____

_____

_____

_____

How this passage can be applied to my life:

_____
_____
_____
_____
_____
_____
_____
_____
_____
_____

Memory verse(s) from today's reading:

_____
_____
_____
_____
_____
_____
_____
_____
_____
_____

Now hope does not disappoint, because the love of God has been poured out in our hearts by the Holy Spirit who was given to us.

ROMANS 5:5 NKJV

Key Bible verses: _____

_____
_____
_____
_____
_____
_____
_____
_____
_____

Date:

Notes: _____

_____
_____
_____
_____
_____
_____
_____
_____
_____
_____
_____
_____

How this passage can be applied to my life:

_____
_____
_____
_____
_____
_____
_____
_____
_____
_____
_____

Memory verse(s) from today's reading:

_____
_____
_____
_____
_____
_____
_____
_____
_____
_____
_____

Meditate on these things; give yourself entirely to them,

that your progress may be evident to all.

1 TIMOTHY 4:15 NKJV

Key Bible verses: _____

_____

_____

_____

_____

_____

_____

_____

_____

_____

_____

_____

Date:

Notes: _____

_____

_____

_____

_____

_____

_____

_____

_____

_____

_____

_____

_____

How this passage can be applied to my life:

_____
_____
_____
_____
_____
_____
_____
_____
_____
_____

Memory verse(s) from today's reading:

_____
_____
_____
_____
_____
_____
_____
_____
_____
_____

I wait for the LORD, my soul doth wait,
and in his word do I hope.

PSALM 130:5 KJV

Key Bible verses: _____

_____
_____
_____
_____
_____
_____
_____
_____

Notes: _____

_____
_____
_____
_____
_____
_____
_____
_____
_____
_____
_____

Date: _____

How this passage can be applied to my life:

_____
_____
_____
_____
_____
_____
_____
_____
_____
_____
_____

Memory verse(s) from today's reading:

_____
_____
_____
_____
_____
_____
_____
_____
_____
_____
_____

My soul followeth hard after thee: thy right hand upholdeth me.

PSALM 63:8 KJV

Key Bible verses: _____

_____
_____
_____
_____
_____
_____
_____
_____
_____
_____

Date:

Notes: _____

_____
_____
_____
_____
_____
_____
_____
_____
_____
_____
_____
_____
_____

How this passage can be applied to my life:

_____

_____

_____

_____

_____

_____

_____

_____

_____

_____

Memory verse(s) from today's reading:

_____

_____

_____

_____

_____

_____

_____

_____

_____

_____

For the LORD knows the way of the righteous,
but the way of the ungodly shall perish.

PSALM 1:6 NKJV

Key Bible verses: _____

_____

_____

_____

_____

_____

_____

_____

_____

_____

_____

Date: _____

Notes: _____

_____

_____

_____

_____

_____

_____

_____

_____

_____

_____

_____

_____

_____

How this passage can be applied to my life:

_____

_____

_____

_____

_____

_____

_____

_____

_____

_____

Memory verse(s) from today's reading:

_____

_____

_____

_____

_____

_____

_____

_____

_____

For I know whom I have believed, and am persuaded that he is able to keep that which I have committed unto him against that day.

2 TIMOTHY 1:12 KJV

Key Bible verses: _____

_____
_____
_____
_____
_____
_____
_____
_____
_____
_____
_____

Date: _____

Notes: _____

_____
_____
_____
_____
_____
_____
_____
_____
_____
_____
_____
_____
_____
_____

How this passage can be applied to my life:

_____

_____

_____

_____

_____

_____

_____

_____

_____

_____

_____

Memory verse(s) from today's reading:

_____

_____

_____

_____

_____

_____

_____

_____

_____

_____

_____

*"You shall love the LORD your God with all your heart
and with all your soul and with all your might."*

DEUTERONOMY 6:5 NASB

Key Bible verses: _____

_____
_____
_____
_____
_____
_____
_____
_____
_____
_____
_____

Date: _____

Notes: _____

_____
_____
_____
_____
_____
_____
_____
_____
_____
_____
_____
_____

How this passage can be applied to my life:

_____
_____
_____
_____
_____
_____
_____
_____
_____
_____

Memory verse(s) from today's reading:

_____
_____
_____
_____
_____
_____
_____
_____
_____
_____
_____

For such is the will of God that by doing right you may silence the ignorance of foolish men.

1 PETER 2:15 NASB

Key Bible verses: _____

_____
_____
_____
_____
_____
_____
_____
_____
_____
_____
_____

Date: _____

Notes: _____

_____
_____
_____
_____
_____
_____
_____
_____
_____
_____
_____
_____
_____
_____

How this passage can be applied to my life:

Memory verse(s) from today's reading:

Your words were found and I ate them,
and Your words became for me a joy and the delight of my heart.

JEREMIAH 15:16 NASB

Key Bible verses: _____

_____
_____
_____
_____
_____
_____
_____
_____
_____
_____

Date:

Notes: _____

_____
_____
_____
_____
_____
_____
_____
_____
_____
_____
_____
_____
_____

How this passage can be applied to my life:

_____
_____
_____
_____
_____
_____
_____
_____
_____
_____
_____

Memory verse(s) from today's reading:

_____
_____
_____
_____
_____
_____
_____
_____
_____
_____
_____

Prove yourselves to be blameless and innocent, children of God above reproach in the midst of a crooked and perverse generation, among whom you appear as lights in the world, holding fast the word of life.

PHILIPPIANS 2:15–16 NASB

Key Bible verses: _____

_____
_____
_____
_____
_____
_____
_____
_____
_____
_____

Date: _____

Notes: _____

_____
_____
_____
_____
_____
_____
_____
_____
_____
_____
_____
_____
_____

How this passage can be applied to my life:

_____
_____
_____
_____
_____
_____
_____
_____
_____
_____

Memory verse(s) from today's reading:

_____
_____
_____
_____
_____
_____
_____
_____
_____
_____
_____

Those who seek the LORD understand all things.

PROVERBS 28:5 NASB

Key Bible verses: _____

Date: _____

Notes: _____

How this passage can be applied to my life:

_____
_____
_____
_____
_____
_____
_____
_____
_____
_____

Memory verse(s) from today's reading:

_____
_____
_____
_____
_____
_____
_____
_____
_____
_____
_____

My soul clings to the dust; revive me according to Your word.

PSALM 119:25 NKJV

Key Bible verses: _____

Date: ___

_____
_____
_____
_____
_____
_____
_____
_____
_____
_____

Notes: _____

_____
_____
_____
_____
_____
_____
_____
_____
_____
_____
_____
_____
_____

How this passage can be applied to my life:

_____
_____
_____
_____
_____
_____
_____
_____
_____
_____
_____

Memory verse(s) from today's reading:

_____
_____
_____
_____
_____
_____
_____
_____
_____
_____
_____

For this God is our God for ever and ever:
he will be our guide even unto death.

PSALM 48:14 KJV

Key Bible verses: _____

_____
_____
_____
_____
_____
_____
_____
_____
_____
_____

Date: _____

Notes: _____

_____
_____
_____
_____
_____
_____
_____
_____
_____
_____
_____
_____
_____

How this passage can be applied to my life:

_____

_____

_____

_____

_____

_____

_____

_____

_____

_____

_____

_____

Memory verse(s) from today's reading:

_____

_____

_____

_____

_____

_____

_____

_____

_____

_____

_____

_____

Who is the man that fears the LORD?
Him shall He teach in the way He chooses.

PSALM 25:12 NKJV

Key Bible verses: _____

_____

_____

_____

_____

_____

_____

_____

_____

_____

_____

Date:

Notes: _____

_____

_____

_____

_____

_____

_____

_____

_____

_____

_____

_____

_____

_____

_____

How this passage can be applied to my life:

_____
_____
_____
_____
_____
_____
_____
_____
_____
_____
_____
_____

Memory verse(s) from today's reading:

_____
_____
_____
_____
_____
_____
_____
_____
_____
_____
_____
_____

"Master, we have toiled all night and caught nothing;
nevertheless at Your word I will let down the net."

LUKE 5:5 NKJV

Date:

Key Bible verses: _____

_____
_____
_____
_____
_____
_____
_____
_____

Notes: _____

_____
_____
_____
_____
_____
_____
_____
_____
_____
_____
_____

How this passage can be applied to my life:

_____
_____
_____
_____
_____
_____
_____
_____
_____
_____
_____
_____

Memory verse(s) from today's reading:

_____
_____
_____
_____
_____
_____
_____
_____
_____
_____
_____
_____

These things have I written unto you that believe on the name
of the Son of God: that ye may know that ye have eternal life,
and that ye may believe on the name of the Son of God.

1 JOHN 5:13 KJV

Key Bible verses: _____

_____
_____
_____
_____
_____
_____
_____
_____
_____

Date:

Notes: _____

_____
_____
_____
_____
_____
_____
_____
_____
_____
_____
_____
_____

How this passage can be applied to my life:

_____
_____
_____
_____
_____
_____
_____
_____
_____
_____

Memory verse(s) from today's reading:

_____
_____
_____
_____
_____
_____
_____
_____
_____
_____

"No man ever spoke like this Man!"

JOHN 7:46 NKJV

Key Bible verses: _____

_____

_____

_____

_____

_____

_____

_____

_____

_____

Date:

Notes: _____

_____

_____

_____

_____

_____

_____

_____

_____

_____

_____

_____

How this passage can be applied to my life:

_____
_____
_____
_____
_____
_____
_____
_____
_____
_____
_____

Memory verse(s) from today's reading:

_____
_____
_____
_____
_____
_____
_____
_____
_____
_____
_____

"Remain in me, and I will remain in you."

JOHN 15:4 NIV

Key Bible verses: _____

_____

_____

_____

_____

_____

_____

_____

_____

_____

Date:

Notes: _____

_____

_____

_____

_____

_____

_____

_____

_____

_____

_____

_____

_____

How this passage can be applied to my life:

_____

_____

_____

_____

_____

_____

_____

_____

_____

_____

_____

Memory verse(s) from today's reading:

_____

_____

_____

_____

_____

_____

_____

_____

_____

_____

_____

_____

Blessed is the man who finds wisdom, the man who gains understanding.

PROVERBS 3:13 NIV

Key Bible verses: _____

_____

_____

_____

_____

_____

_____

_____

_____

_____

_____

Date: _____

Notes: _____

_____

_____

_____

_____

_____

_____

_____

_____

_____

_____

_____

_____

How this passage can be applied to my life:

_____

_____

_____

_____

_____

_____

_____

_____

_____

_____

Memory verse(s) from today's reading:

_____

_____

_____

_____

_____

_____

_____

_____

_____

_____

For yet in a very little while, He who is coming will come, and will not delay.

HEBREWS 10:37 NASB

Date: _____

Key Bible verses: _____

_____
_____
_____
_____
_____
_____
_____
_____
_____
_____

Notes: _____

_____
_____
_____
_____
_____
_____
_____
_____
_____
_____
_____
_____
_____

How this passage can be applied to my life:

_____
_____
_____
_____
_____
_____
_____
_____
_____
_____
_____

Memory verse(s) from today's reading:

_____
_____
_____
_____
_____
_____
_____
_____
_____
_____
_____

The words of the LORD are pure words:
as silver tried in a furnace on the earth, refined seven times.

PSALM 12:6 NASB

Key Bible verses: _____

Date:

Notes: _____

How this passage can be applied to my life:

_____
_____
_____
_____
_____
_____
_____
_____
_____
_____
_____

Memory verse(s) from today's reading:

_____
_____
_____
_____
_____
_____
_____
_____
_____
_____

"Blessed is the man who listens to me,

watching daily at my gates, waiting at my doorposts."

PROVERBS 8:34 NASB

Key Bible verses: _____

_____

_____

_____

_____

_____

_____

_____

_____

_____

Date: _____

Notes: _____

_____

_____

_____

_____

_____

_____

_____

_____

_____

_____

_____

How this passage can be applied to my life:

_____
_____
_____
_____
_____
_____
_____
_____
_____
_____
_____

Memory verse(s) from today's reading:

_____
_____
_____
_____
_____
_____
_____
_____
_____
_____
_____
_____

Lead me in thy truth, and teach me: for thou art the God of my salvation.

Key Bible verses: _____
_____
_____
_____
_____
_____
_____
_____
_____
_____
_____

Date: _____

Notes: _____
_____
_____
_____
_____
_____
_____
_____
_____
_____
_____
_____
_____

How this passage can be applied to my life:

_____
_____
_____
_____
_____
_____
_____
_____
_____
_____
_____

Memory verse(s) from today's reading:

_____
_____
_____
_____
_____
_____
_____
_____
_____
_____
_____

When I sit in darkness, the LORD shall be a light unto me.

MICAH 7:8 KJV

Key Bible verses: _____

_____
_____
_____
_____
_____
_____
_____
_____
_____
_____
_____
_____

Date: _____

Notes: _____

_____
_____
_____
_____
_____
_____
_____
_____
_____
_____
_____
_____
_____

How this passage can be applied to my life:

_____

_____

_____

_____

_____

_____

_____

_____

_____

_____

Memory verse(s) from today's reading:

_____

_____

_____

_____

_____

_____

_____

_____

_____

_____

_____

I will stand on my guard post and station myself on the rampart;
and I will keep watch to see what He will speak to me.

HABAKKUK 2:1 NASB

Date: _____

Key Bible verses: _____

_____
_____
_____
_____
_____
_____
_____
_____
_____
_____
_____

Notes: _____

_____
_____
_____
_____
_____
_____
_____
_____
_____
_____
_____
_____

How this passage can be applied to my life:

_____
_____
_____
_____
_____
_____
_____
_____
_____
_____
_____
_____

Memory verse(s) from today's reading:

_____
_____
_____
_____
_____
_____
_____
_____
_____
_____
_____

*"What I tell you in the darkness, speak in the light;
and what you hear whispered in your ear, proclaim upon the housetops."*

MATTHEW 10:27 NASB

Key Bible verses: _____

_____

_____

_____

_____

_____

_____

_____

_____

_____

_____

Date:

Notes: _____

_____

_____

_____

_____

_____

_____

_____

_____

_____

_____

_____

_____

_____

How this passage can be applied to my life:

_____
_____
_____
_____
_____
_____
_____
_____
_____
_____
_____

Memory verse(s) from today's reading:

_____
_____
_____
_____
_____
_____
_____
_____
_____
_____
_____
_____

Thy hands have made me and fashioned me:
give me understanding, that I may learn thy commandments.

PSALM 119:73 KJV

Key Bible verses: _____

_____

_____

_____

_____

_____

_____

_____

_____

_____

_____

Date:

Notes: _____

_____

_____

_____

_____

_____

_____

_____

_____

_____

_____

_____

_____

_____

How this passage can be applied to my life:

_____

_____

_____

_____

_____

_____

_____

_____

_____

_____

_____

Memory verse(s) from today's reading:

_____

_____

_____

_____

_____

_____

_____

_____

_____

_____

_____

"But for you who revere my name,
the sun of righteousness will rise with healing in its wings."

MALACHI 4:2 NIV

Key Bible verses: _____
_____
_____
_____
_____
_____
_____
_____
_____
_____
_____

Date: _____

Notes: _____
_____
_____
_____
_____
_____
_____
_____
_____
_____
_____
_____
_____
_____

How this passage can be applied to my life:

_____
_____
_____
_____
_____
_____
_____
_____
_____
_____
_____

Memory verse(s) from today's reading:

_____
_____
_____
_____
_____
_____
_____
_____
_____
_____
_____
_____
_____
_____

The LORD revealed himself to Samuel in Shiloh
by the word of the LORD.

1 SAMUEL 3:21 KJV

Date:

Key Bible verses: _____

_____
_____
_____
_____
_____
_____
_____
_____
_____
_____

Notes: _____

_____
_____
_____
_____
_____
_____
_____
_____
_____
_____
_____
_____
_____
_____

How this passage can be applied to my life:

_____

_____

_____

_____

_____

_____

_____

_____

_____

_____

_____

Memory verse(s) from today's reading:

_____

_____

_____

_____

_____

_____

_____

_____

_____

_____

_____

_____

_____

But the word of God grew and multiplied.

ACTS 12:24 KJV

Key Bible verses: _____

_____
_____
_____
_____
_____
_____
_____
_____
_____

Date: _____

Notes: _____

_____
_____
_____
_____
_____
_____
_____
_____
_____
_____
_____

How this passage can be applied to my life:

_____
_____
_____
_____
_____
_____
_____
_____
_____
_____
_____
_____

Memory verse(s) from today's reading:

_____
_____
_____
_____
_____
_____
_____
_____
_____
_____
_____
_____

And take the helmet of salvation, and the sword of the Spirit,
which is the word of God.

EPHESIANS 6:17 KJV

Key Bible verses: _____

_____

_____

_____

_____

_____

_____

_____

_____

Date:

Notes: _____

_____

_____

_____

_____

_____

_____

_____

_____

_____

_____

_____

How this passage can be applied to my life:

_____
_____
_____
_____
_____
_____
_____
_____
_____
_____
_____

Memory verse(s) from today's reading:

_____
_____
_____
_____
_____
_____
_____
_____
_____
_____
_____

Whoso despiseth the word shall be destroyed:
but he that feareth the commandment shall be rewarded.

PROVERBS 13:13 KJV

Key Bible verses: _____

_____
_____
_____
_____
_____
_____
_____
_____
_____

Notes: _____

_____
_____
_____
_____
_____
_____
_____
_____
_____
_____

Date: _____

How this passage can be applied to my life:

_____
_____
_____
_____
_____
_____
_____
_____
_____
_____
_____
_____

Memory verse(s) from today's reading:

_____
_____
_____
_____
_____
_____
_____
_____
_____
_____
_____
_____

Heaven and earth shall pass away: but my words shall not pass away.

MARK 13:31 KJV

Key Bible verses: _____

_____
_____
_____
_____
_____
_____
_____
_____
_____

Date:

Notes: _____

_____
_____
_____
_____
_____
_____
_____
_____
_____
_____
_____
_____

How this passage can be applied to my life:

Memory verse(s) from today's reading:

"And the gospel must first be preached to all nations."

MARK 13:10 NIV

Key Bible verses: _____

_____
_____
_____
_____
_____
_____
_____
_____
_____

Date:

Notes: _____

_____
_____
_____
_____
_____
_____
_____
_____
_____
_____
_____

How this passage can be applied to my life:

_____
_____
_____
_____
_____
_____
_____
_____
_____
_____
_____

Memory verse(s) from today's reading:

_____
_____
_____
_____
_____
_____
_____
_____
_____
_____
_____

In the beginning was the Word, and the Word was with God, and the Word was God.

JOHN 1:1 KJV

Date:

Key Bible verses: _____

_____

_____

_____

_____

_____

_____

_____

_____

_____

_____

Notes: _____

_____

_____

_____

_____

_____

_____

_____

_____

_____

_____

_____

_____

How this passage can be applied to my life:

_____
_____
_____
_____
_____
_____
_____
_____
_____
_____
_____

Memory verse(s) from today's reading:

_____
_____
_____
_____
_____
_____
_____
_____
_____
_____
_____
_____

"Everything must be fulfilled that is written about me in the Law of Moses, the Prophets and the Psalms."

LUKE 24:44 NIV

Date:

Key Bible verses: _____

_____
_____
_____
_____
_____
_____
_____
_____
_____
_____

Notes: _____

_____
_____
_____
_____
_____
_____
_____
_____
_____
_____
_____
_____

How this passage can be applied to my life:

_____
_____
_____
_____
_____
_____
_____
_____
_____
_____

Memory verse(s) from today's reading:

_____
_____
_____
_____
_____
_____
_____
_____
_____
_____
_____

I, Paul, write this greeting in my own hand.

COLOSSIANS 4:18 NIV

Key Bible verses: _____

_____
_____
_____
_____
_____
_____
_____
_____
_____
_____
_____

Date:

Notes: _____

_____
_____
_____
_____
_____
_____
_____
_____
_____
_____
_____
_____
_____

How this passage can be applied to my life:

_____
_____
_____
_____
_____
_____
_____
_____
_____
_____

Memory verse(s) from today's reading:

_____
_____
_____
_____
_____
_____
_____
_____
_____
_____

For you have been born again, not of perishable seed,
but of imperishable, through the living and enduring word of God.

1 PETER 1:23 NIV

Key Bible verses: _____

Date:

Notes: _____

How this passage can be applied to my life:

_____
_____
_____
_____
_____
_____
_____
_____
_____
_____
_____

Memory verse(s) from today's reading:

_____
_____
_____
_____
_____
_____
_____
_____
_____
_____
_____

The grass withereth, and the flower thereof falleth away:
but the word of the Lord endureth forever.

1 PETER 1:24–25 KJV

Key Bible verses: _____

_____

_____

_____

_____

_____

_____

_____

_____

_____

Date:

Notes: _____

_____

_____

_____

_____

_____

_____

_____

_____

_____

_____

How this passage can be applied to my life:

_____
_____
_____
_____
_____
_____
_____
_____
_____
_____

Memory verse(s) from today's reading:

_____
_____
_____
_____
_____
_____
_____
_____
_____
_____

Preach the Word; be prepared in season and out of season.

2 TIMOTHY 4:2 NIV

Key Bible verses: _____

_____
_____
_____
_____
_____
_____
_____
_____
_____

Date:

Notes: _____

_____
_____
_____
_____
_____
_____
_____
_____
_____
_____
_____
_____
_____